WITHDRAWN

NORTH AMERICAN NATURAL RESOURCES

MARINE RESOURCES

North American Natural Resources

Coal
Copper
Freshwater Resources
Gold and Silver
Iron
Marine Resources
Natural Gas
Oil
Renewable Energy
Salt
Timber and Forest Products
Uranium

NORTH AMERICAN NATURAL RESOURCES

MARINE RESOURCES

LONDON PUBLIC LIBRARY

John Perritano

MASON CREST

Mason Crest
450 Parkway Drive, Suite D
Broomall, PA 19008
www.masoncrest.com

© 2016 by Mason Crest, an imprint of National Highlights, Inc. All rights reserved. No part of this publication may be reproduced or transmitted in any form or by any means, electronic or mechanical, including photocopying, recording, taping, or any information storage and retrieval system, without permission from the publisher.

MTM Publishing, Inc.
435 West 23rd Street, #8C
New York, NY 10011
www.mtmpublishing.com

President: Valerie Tomaselli
Vice President, Book Development: Hilary Poole
Designer: Annemarie Redmond
Illustrator: Richard Garratt
Copyeditor: Peter Jaskowiak
Editorial Assistant: Andrea St. Aubin

Series ISBN: 978-1-4222-3378-8
ISBN: 978-1-4222-3384-9
Ebook ISBN: 978-1-4222-8558-9

Library of Congress Cataloging-in-Publication Data
Perritano, John.
  Marine Resources / by John Perritano.
      pages cm. — (North American natural resources)
  Includes bibliographical references and index.
  ISBN 978-1-4222-3384-9 (hardback) — ISBN 978-1-4222-3378-8 (series)—ISBN 978-1-4222-8558-9 (ebook)
  1. Marine resources—Juvenile literature. I. Title.
  GC1025.G37 2015
  333.91'6416—dc23
                                    2015005843

Printed and bound in the United States of America.

First printing
9 8 7 6 5 4 3 2 1

TABLE OF CONTENTS

Introduction 7
Chapter One: Formation and Location 9
Chapter Two: Ecosystems 18
Chapter Three: Science and Uses 27
Chapter Four: Environment 37
Chapter Five: Protection 47
Further Reading 57
Series Glossary 58
Index 60
About the Author 64
Photo Credits 64

Key Icons to Look for:

Words to Understand: These words with their easy-to-understand definitions will increase the reader's understanding of the text, while building vocabulary skills.

Sidebars: This boxed material within the main text allows readers to build knowledge, gain insights, explore possibilities, and broaden their perspectives by weaving together additional information to provide realistic and holistic perspectives.

Research Projects: Readers are pointed toward areas of further inquiry connected to each chapter. Suggestions are provided for projects that encourage deeper research and analysis.

Text-Dependent Questions: These questions send the reader back to the text for more careful attention to the evidence presented there.

Series Glossary of Key Terms: This back-of-the-book glossary contains terminology used throughout the series. Words found here increase the reader's ability to read and comprehend higher-level books and articles in this field.

Note to Educator: As publishers, we feel it's our role to give young adults the tools they need to thrive in a global society. To encourage a more worldly perspective, this book contains both imperial and metric measurements as well as references to a wider global context. We hope to expose the readers to the most common conversions they will come across outside of North America.

North American Marine Resources

- Site Mentioned in Text

- Arctic National Wildlife Refuge
- Gilbert Bay
- Davis Strait
- Hudson Bay
- Gulf of St. Lawrence
- Bay of Fundy
- Gulf of Maine
- Narragansett Bay
- Delmarva Peninsula
- Chesapeake Bay
- San Francisco Bay
- Tijuana River Watershed
- Florida Keys Reef System
- Clam Bayou
- Gulf of Mexico
- Puerto Rico Trench
- Yucatán Peninsula
- Caribbean Sea
- Prudhoe Bay
- Prince William Sound
- Dutch Harbor

CANADA
UNITED STATES OF AMERICA
MEXICO

PACIFIC OCEAN
ATLANTIC OCEAN

INTRODUCTION

The oceans are immense and beautiful, dangerous and mysterious. They are filled with food, energy, and other riches. Yet oceans are more than that. The oceans play a key role in regulating Earth's climate. They remove carbon dioxide (CO_2) from the atmosphere and provide the planet with half of its life-sustaining oxygen. They regulate weather patterns and cleanse the environment of poisons. Indeed, we depend on the oceans for our very survival.

A view of the Pacific Ocean off the coast of California. (Imdan/Dreamstime)

The oceans are where life evolved billions of years ago, and where both the largest and smallest animals now live. People have feasted on this bounty for thousands of years. Even today, more than one billion people obtain most of their protein from the oceans.

We play in the oceans. We travel above and beneath them. We use ocean waves to generate electricity. We drill below the marine floor looking for oil to run our homes, automobiles, and factories. The ocean is so important to our lives that nearly half of the world's 7 billion people live close to one ocean or another.

Yet we know so little about the oceans. They remain largely unexplored and are the last true frontiers on Earth. However, we do know that human activities influence the health of the oceans. Human activities, particularly the burning of fossil fuels, have affected global weather patterns. Polar ice sheets are melting and the oceans are rising. We also use the world's oceans as a dumping ground for sewage, chemicals, and other forms of pollution, including nuclear waste. Although they are immense, the oceans are fragile. If we ruin them, we ruin ourselves.

Chapter One

FORMATION AND LOCATION

For years, Darren Stander worked alongside several other fishermen plying the waters of the Gulf of Mexico searching for crabs and oysters. Everyone made a good living. That all changed in 2010, when one of the worst marine disasters in US history rocked the Gulf of Mexico. On April 20, a massive explosion onboard an oil-drilling platform killed 11 workers and caused 210 million gallons (almost 800 million liters) of crude oil to spill into the water.

Words to Understand

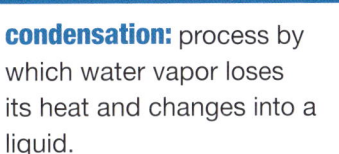

condensation: process by which water vapor loses its heat and changes into a liquid.

estuary: a body of water where freshwater meets the sea.

habitats: environments for animals and plants.

oozes: deep sea sediments.

salinity: amount of salt in a substance.

tectonic plates: landmasses that float on Earth's crust.

Marine Resources

The oil drifted far from the rig, soiling vast stretches of Gulf Coast beaches. It took workers three months to cap the gusher, and many more to ease the environmental damage. Much of the crude washed ashore, fouling 1,100 miles (1,770.28 kilometers) of coastline from Florida to Mississippi. Some of the oil settled on the bottom of the ocean, destroying local fishing grounds.

Before the spill, about two-thirds of all the oysters in the United States came from the Gulf of Mexico. After the explosion, the oyster reefs grew barren and other fish were tougher to find. The catastrophe reminded people just how valuable marine resources are, and how much we humans depend on the oceans for our survival.

The Deepwater Horizon rig burns after a massive explosion on April 20, 2010.

The western hemisphere of Earth, photographed from space. Photographs like this one lead to the Earth being nicknamed "the Big Blue Marble" because of its vast oceans.

A Unique Planet

In many ways, the planet Earth is in a class of its own. For one thing, no other planet in our solar system has vast oceans of water that sustain life. Earth has so much ocean water that if you were to mold the planet's surface it into a smooth sphere with no mountains or valleys, that sphere would be completely covered by seawater nearly 8,200 feet (2,500 meters) deep.

Oceans by the Numbers

Earth has five oceans: Pacific, Atlantic, Indian, Arctic, and Antarctic (sometimes called Southern).
- **Area**—Pacific: 64.1 million square miles (165.2 square kilometers); Atlantic: 41 million square miles (106 million square kilometers); Indian: 28.3 million square miles (73.5 million square kilometers); Arctic: 5.4 million square miles (14.06 square kilometers); Antarctic: 7.848 million square miles (20.33 square million kilometers).
- **Deepest Points**—Pacific: Mariana Trench, 35,840 feet (10,924.03 meters); Atlantic: Puerto Rico Trench, 28,232 feet (8,605.11 meters); Indian: Java Trench, 23,376 feet (7,125.00 meters).

The Earth wasn't always so wet, however. About 4 billion years ago, the planet was a vast wasteland, a bubbling cauldron of hot rock. Eventually, exploding stars, along with comets and asteroids slamming into the planet, seeded Earth with organic elements, including hydrogen and oxygen, the two main ingredients in water.

Over time, volcanoes spewed hydrogen and oxygen from deep inside the Earth. They combined to create water vapor and an atmosphere. As the Earth cooled, the **condensation** fell in the forms of rain, snow, and hail, creating the oceans.

The world's oceans contain roughly 3.2 billion cubic miles (1.35 billion cubic kilometers) of seawater that varies in temperature, **salinity**, and pressure. Under all this water are vast mountain ranges, deep trenches, and coral—the largest structure built by a living organism. The oceans are **habitats** that provide fertile ground for various species of plants and animals. Precious metals such as gold and copper are buried deep in the sea muck.

North American Oceans

North America is surrounded by water. It is flanked by the Pacific Ocean in the west, the Atlantic Ocean in the east, and the Arctic Ocean in the north. Canada has the largest coastline in the world, totaling 125,566.69 miles (202,080 kilometers). The United States has the world's 9th largest coastline, with 12,380.20 miles (19,924 kilometers); and Mexico is 15th, with 5,797.39 miles (9,330 kilometers) of coastline. The Pacific is Earth's largest ocean, covering more than a third of Earth's surface, with an area of more than 60 million square miles (156 million square kilometers). The ocean also contains the deepest point on the planet, the Challenger Deep in the Mariana Trench.

The story of North America, its coastline, and its oceans began more than 200 million years ago, when Earth had only one continent, called Pangaea, and one ocean, called Panthalassa. Pangaea was made up of several landmasses that eventually separated as Earth's **tectonic plates** rolled across the crust. As these plates drifted further apart, the continents and the oceans that are so familiar to us today formed.

Bays and Gulfs

Geologically speaking, North America is always on the go, shifting one way, moving another. Occasionally, its landscape is bombarded with comets and asteroids, scarring the land forever. Such was the case about 35 million years ago, when a large comet-like object crashed into what is today the Delmarva Peninsula, near Cape Charles, Virginia.

The collision created a crater the size of Rhode Island. The impact, coupled with the carving ability of retreating glaciers some 18,000 years ago, formed Chesapeake

A few of the many shrimp boats that work the Gulf of Mexico.

14 Marine Resources

Satellite image of Chesapeake Bay.

Oceans on the Go

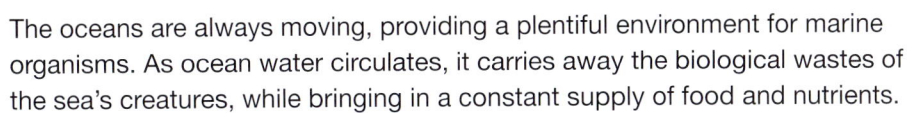

The oceans are always moving, providing a plentiful environment for marine organisms. As ocean water circulates, it carries away the biological wastes of the sea's creatures, while bringing in a constant supply of food and nutrients.

The wind moves the upper layers of the ocean, creating waves and surface currents. Some of these currents carry warm water away from the equator and cold water toward it. One of these currents is the Gulf Stream, which flows out of the warm Gulf of Mexico northward across the cooler Atlantic. It influences weather patterns as far away as Europe. The gravitational pull of the moon and sun, along with shifts in the movement of Earth's crust, also help move ocean water.

Bay, a 200-mile **estuary** where salt water and freshwater mix. Glaciers also helped form Hudson Bay in northeastern Canada.

North America is also home to several gulfs, which are large inlets of ocean. The largest is the Gulf of Mexico, which borders six southeastern states and nearly all of northeastern Mexico including the states of Tamaulipas, Veracruz, Tabasco, Campeche, and Yucatán. It also borders the island-nation of Cuba to the southeast. The Gulf of Mexico formed around 300 million years ago and is one of the largest bodies in of water in the world. The Gulf of Mexico, like many other gulfs, formed when Earth's tectonic plates began to rift, or break apart. The Gulf of Mexico formed when Pangaea split and created two supercontinents. One was Laurasia, which itself split into North America and Eurasia, and the other was Gondwana, which is now South America and Africa. As the two moved farther apart, they created the Gulf.

These days, the Gulf of Mexico is rich in life, especially around the west coast of Florida, where the currents bring cold, nutrient-rich water to the ocean surface. Many different types of fish and organisms live in the region. The warm Gulf waters also influence weather patterns by allowing storms to gather strength; this is why Florida, Texas, Louisiana, and Cuba are often hit by hurricanes and tropical storms.

Parts of the Ocean Floor

An abundance of marine resources lie on the ocean floor, which begins in a shallow area known as the continental shelf. The continental shelf sits just off the continent and gradually slopes downward. At the end of that shelf is the so-called continental slope, the boundary between the edge of the continent and the ocean floor.

On the floor of the ocean are a variety of terrain, including plains, ridges, and trenches. The deepest place on the planet is the Mariana Trench in the western part of the North Pacific. Inside the trench is a place called the Challenger Deep, which is more than 35,000 feet (almost 11,000 meters) deep.

The oceans also include some of the highest mountains on the planet. Mauna Kea, a dormant volcano in Hawaii, is taller than Mount Everest. When measured from its base at the bottom of the Pacific to its summit, Mauna Kea is more than 32,000 feet (about 10,000 meters) tall, much higher than Everest, which is 29,035 feet (8,850 meters) high.

For the most part, the seafloor is covered in layers of mud hundreds of feet deep. The mud provides a thriving environment for many different plants and animals. The mud contains **oozes**, or the remains of organic material from dead plants and animals. These oozes serve as prime feeding grounds for unusual marine life.

The view from the summit of Mauna Kea.

TEXT-DEPENDENT QUESTIONS

1. What are the names of the vast continent and sea that covered the early world?
2. What is the highest mountain in the world?
3. What is the deepest point on Earth?

RESEARCH PROJECT

Map the flow of the Gulf Stream and research how it impacts weather systems.

Chapter Two

ECOSYSTEMS

Words to Understand

algae: photosynthetic organisms that are usually one-celled organisms.

biotoxin: a poisonous substance produced by a living organism.

chlorophyll: green pigment found in algae and plants that absorbs sunlight.

estuary: the mouth of a river.

intertidal zones: the seashore.

mangroves: tropical trees with shallow roots that grow in or near water.

The oceans are where life on Earth began, and they are what sustains life today. Without the oceans, humans would literally run out of air to breathe. Like all ecosystems, where plants and animals interact with their environment, aquatic ecosystems are very complex and have many parts. When marine habitats are harmed, it can affect the entire planet.

Coral reefs, **estuaries**, **mangrove** forests, the sea floor, salt marshes, and **intertidal zones**, also known as the seashore, are all different types of marine ecosystems. More than one million species of plants and animals live in the ocean, and scientists believe there are millions more that have yet to be identified.

Important Algae

One of the most important parts of a marine ecosystem is **algae**, also known as *phytoplankton*. Phytoplankton are microscopic algae that contain **chlorophyll** and need sunlight to live and grow. These tiny creatures live near the surface of the water

The Pacific Ocean as seen from space; the milky blue areas are an enormous algal bloom off the coast of Japan.

so they can soak up the sun. Phytoplankton are the primary source of food for most animals in the ocean, from tiny fish to massive whales.

Phytoplankton serve another purpose as well—without them, it would be impossible for humans to breathe. Like all plants, algae take in huge of amounts of carbon dioxide, and they release oxygen. Phytoplankton produce most of the oxygen on the planet.

But while phytoplankton sustain life, they can also bring death and disease in the form of red tides. A red tide is a harmful algal bloom, a rapid increase in the population of algae created when certain species of phytoplankton produce powerful **biotoxins**. These poisons can paralyze a creature's nervous system and harm people who inhale the toxins when the wind blows them onshore.

These blooms can take on eerie colors, including red, yellow, and green. Most algal blooms are the result of excess nutrients, particularly nitrogen and phosphorus, in the water, which causes algae to grow rapidly. In 2013, a red tide infected the grasses eaten by manatees in Florida. The result was the death of 276 of the endangered animals. In 2014, a toxic red tide began killing sea turtles, fish, and sharks in the Gulf of Mexico just off the coast of Florida.

Coral Reefs

Coral reefs are another example of a marine ecosystem. The reefs provide shelter and food for thousands of species of sea creatures, while also protecting the shoreline from waves and storms. Corals might look like simple rocks, but in fact they are tiny, soft-bodied animals that build chalky limestone skeletons to protect themselves. These skeletons cement themselves together and build up over time to form reefs. The reefs contain millions of coral animals known as *polyps*.

Corals have a beneficial relationship with many other animals. These animals rely on corals as a source of food and shelter. Many kinds of sea creatures, such as star fish, sea urchins, and sea turtles, depend on corals for their survival. At the same time, coral reefs provide a nursery for thousands of different animal species. Coral reefs also deflect the power of oncoming waves created by hurricanes, typhoons, and tsunamis. A healthy reef can grow 7.87 inches (20 centimeters) a year. The Florida Keys reef

Staghorn coral.

system is the largest living coral reef in North America, covering some 221 miles (355.67 kilometers) along Florida's southeast coast.

Coral reefs are in danger, however. Climate change, which involves a gradual increase in Earth's surface temperature, has warmed waters and destroyed many species of coral around the world. So it was with some surprise that, in 2015, scientists in South Florida announced a major discovery. They found 38 acres of staghorn coral. This staghorn coral, which look like tiny deer horns reaching up from the seabed, was a major find because it is slowly disappearing. This particular species is important because of its ability to build coral reefs.

Watersheds

Watersheds are places where all water flows to the same area, much like a funnel. Watersheds are separated from one another by ridges, hills, or mountains. Watersheds come in many sizes, and there are 2,110 of them in the continental United States, and more than 2,000 more in Alaska, Hawaii, and Puerto Rico. The Mississippi watershed is the largest watershed in North America. It is made up of the Missouri, Arkansas, Ohio, and Tennessee Rivers. The water from those areas empties into the Gulf of Mexico.

Canada's water drains into the Arctic, Pacific, and Atlantic Oceans from five main watersheds. Nearly 30 percent of Canada's water drains to the Hudson Bay watershed

The Mississippi River flows into the Gulf of Mexico.

A Tasty Filter

Chesapeake Bay is famous for its oysters, but overharvesting, disease, and the loss of habitat has decimated the population. Scientists have been working hard for years to reverse the decline. That's because oysters are important to the health of the planet. Oysters are tiny water filters. As they feed, they pump water through their gills, trapping contaminants. A single oyster can filter more than 50 gallons of water (189 liters) a day. When the Chesapeake brimmed with oysters in the late 1800s, the creatures could filter all the water in the bay in four days. Today, the same job takes a year.

Oysters are prized for eating, but they are also vital to the health of watersheds like the Chesapeake Bay.

and into the Arctic Ocean. In eastern Canada, most water passes through the Great Lakes–St. Lawrence watershed into the Atlantic.

The Tijuana River watershed, which straddles the US–Mexico border, covers 1,750 square miles (4,532 square kilometers), takes water from both countries, and directs it into the Pacific.

Estuaries

Estuaries are places where rivers and oceans meet. In North America, Narragansett Bay and San Fransicsco Bay are two of the largest. But no estuary in North America is as large as Chesapeake Bay. With a shoreline of 8,000 miles (12,800 kilometers), Chesapeake Bay is a complex ecosystem that includes the nearby ocean, rivers, streams, wetlands, and lakes. Half of the water in the bay comes from the Atlantic, while the other half drains through a 64,000-square-mile (165,000-square-kilometer) watershed. The bay supports more than 3,000 species of plants and animals, including 173 species of shellfish.

Chesapeake Bay, like other estuaries, serves as a gigantic filter that removes pollutants such as herbicides, pesticides, and heavy metals from the environment. Marsh grasses and a spongy substance called *peat* (a mixture of decomposing plants, animals, and soil) filter water as it passes through the bay and its other associated habitats, including salt marshes and mangrove forests.

Chesapeake Bay and its surrounding wetlands also stabilize and protect the shoreline from floods and storm surges during hurricanes and other storms. The bay also stops soil from eroding.

Mangrove Swamps

In 2011, volunteers planted thousands of thin mangrove seedlings, hoping to restore the ecosystem of Sanibel's Clam Bayou in Florida. Storms and road construction had cut the bayou off from ocean, turning the area into a gray and desolate wasteland. Within three years, the tiny mangrove seedlings had grown into mature trees. The mangrove plantings were part of a massive project to restore the bayou and reconnect it with the ocean.

"When we did the project, people asked me how long it would take for Clam Bayou to come back," said the conservationist Eric Milbrandt. "My guess was 10 years. But it's come back quicker than that. It's amazing how fast it's come back."

Mangroves are small trees that grow in coastal swamps and along rivers and estuaries in tropical and subtropical climates. Mangroves have dense, tangled roots. Tropical mangrove swamps can be found all along the Gulf Coast and in Mexico. These wetlands love salt and fresh water, which is why mangrove forests generally grow along estuaries where the two meet. Like coral reefs, mangrove forests provide a home for many sea creatures, including shrimp and crab. They also provide a safe haven in which fish and other animals can lay their eggs. One study in Central America and southern North America showed that some fish species are 25 times more likely to live next to coral reefs close to mangrove areas than in areas where the mangroves have been cut down.

Mangrove forests help reduce erosion. The trees also filter out sediments, helping to protect coral reefs and meadows of sea grass. Mangrove roots also trap pollutants from reaching the ocean. Both the east and west coasts of Mexico are home to many mangrove swamps. Twenty-nine mangrove forests are located on the Pacific coast, 27 on the Gulf of Mexico, and 25 on the Yucatán Peninsula, which juts out in the Caribbean Sea.

Mangrove trees.

TEXT-DEPENDENT QUESTIONS

1. Explain how mangroves swamps impact the heath of the environment.
2. Why are coral reefs in danger?
3. What are biotoxins?

RESEARCH PROJECT

Research and map the coral reefs around North America. Then make a list of why the reefs are in danger.

Chapter Three

SCIENCE AND USES

From New England to Canada's Bay of Fundy, cod is king—or it used to be. The fish fed families and helped provide people with jobs and homes. During one year in the 1980s, cod fishermen along North America's eastern coast caught 25,000 tons of the tasty fish.

Words to Understand

commodities: items that are bought and sold.

megawatt: 1 million watts of electricity.

migration: movement from one place to another.

sonar: an instrument that uses sound waves to detect underwater objects.

spawn: to lay eggs.

trawler: a vessel used in trawling, or dragging the seabed with a net, for fish.

But these days, there's not enough cod to go around. The fish's population has been decimated to the point where US officials in 2015 banned cod fishing for six months as scientists try to figure out how to get the population to rebound.

It's a tall order. The Gulf of Maine, situated between New England and Canada, is warming faster than any other place on the planet. The waters of the gulf were always cool, warming on average one degree every two decades or so. In the last 10 years, however, the gulf has warmed one degree every two years. As a result, the cod, which thrive in cooler waters, are leaving for more chilly climes. This **migration** is upsetting the area's fishing industry, not to mention the Gulf of Maine's ecosystem.

"[Cod] are not necessarily showing up in the places that they have in the past," a Maine official told the *New York Times*. "We're seeing movement of stocks often north and eastward."

Cod are not the only species impacted by warmer weather. Warming seas discourage other North American species from spawning, while inspiring others to

Alma, a fishing village on the Bay of Fundy, New Brunswick.

Top Fishing States

Although Americans consume far less fish than they used to, the fishing industry is still big business.

Top Fishing States by Volume of Catch

1. Alaska: 5.3 billion pounds
2. Louisiana: 1.2 billion pounds
3. Virginia: 461.9 million pounds
4. Washington: 420.1 million pounds
5. California: 358.2 million pounds

Top Fishing States by Value of Catch

1. Alaska: $1.7 billion
2. Massachusetts: $618.2 million
3. Maine: $448.5 million
4. Louisiana: $356.6 million
5. Washington: $302 million

spawn at the wrong time. Moreover, freshwater from melting glaciers is affecting plankton, the food of choice for most sea creatures.

Although the oceans provide humans with a bounty of treasures, perhaps no one marine resource has been exploited as much as fish. When the first European settlers arrived in North America some 500 years ago, ample fishing grounds greeted them. As the centuries passed, fishing methods become more exact, and more technical. **Sonar** made it easier to find fish. **Trawlers** caught fish in huge numbers by dragging sizable nets along the seabed or at specific depths. Factory ships were built to catch and process fish in one place. All this technology had a hand in destroying fish populations and ancient ecosystems.

Although fishing is no longer the mainstay of many people's diets, Canadians still consume 8.18 pounds (3.71 kilograms) of fresh and frozen fish each year, while the average American eats 14.4 pounds (6.53 kilograms) of fish and shellfish. In 2012, Americans consumed 4.5 billion pounds (2 billion kilos) of seafood.

Mining for Minerals

Two of the main **commodities** in the oceans are salt and magnesium. Magnesium is used as an ingredient in light-metal alloys. Bromine is another mineral mined from the oceans. It is often used as an insecticide and as a gasoline additive. Gold can also be extracted from the ocean. In fact, one Canadian company is looking to mine the Pacific Ocean off Papua New Guinea, for copper, gold, and zinc.

Commercial fishing is still a vital business for specific locations, including cities and towns in Newfoundland, Labrador, New England, Mexico, and along the Pacific coast, especially in Alaska, where commercial fishermen landed 5.3 billion pounds (2.5 billion kilos) of fish in 2012. The largest fishing port in the United States is Dutch Harbor, Alaska.

Commercial fishermen are not the only people who depend upon this important marine resource. The fishing industry also includes canneries, which process and package seafood; icehouses; restaurants; grocery stores; bait and tackle shops; and fuel stations. Moreover, the oceans are also a playground for recreational fishermen. Whether sailfishing off the coast of Florida or bluefishing off the Connecticut coast, recreational anglers in the United States caught nearly 380 million fish in 2012, most of which were released back into the wild. Sea trout was the most popular recreational fish among saltwater anglers, with more than 43 million of that species caught in 2012. Sea bass, flounder, and red drum were also popular catches.

In the United States, the sport fishing industry supports more than 800,000 jobs, including restaurant and hotel workers, and people who sell fishing tackle, bait, boats, and more. As many as 33 million people, aged 16 or older, go fishing, many in salt water. They spend about $48 million a year on equipment, licenses, and fishing gear.

Aquaculture

Marine aquaculture, or fish farming, is looked upon as a one solution to providing the world with more food. It's also promoted as a way to provide a living for thousands of people who have seen their fishing livelihoods disappear. The term *marine aquaculture* refers to the breeding and harvesting of certain species of fish, such as

The net of a shrimp trawler in the Wadden Sea, in northwestern Europe.

Salmon cages on a fish farm.

salmon, sea bass, char, tuna, and tilapia. Fish farms also raise oysters, clams, mussels, and shrimp. In fact, 40 percent of the seafood people eat today comes from fish farms. It's a $78 billion industry.

Fish farms are located not only in the ocean, but also in coastal areas near inland rivers and lakes. The fish can be raised in large tanks, artificial ponds, or enclosures in the sea itself. However, fish farms pose unique environmental concerns, which will be covered later on in this book.

Energy

Beneath the ocean floor are great reserves of fossil fuels, particularly oil and natural gas. Many of these reserves are located on the outer continental shelf, between the continent and the deep ocean. To extract into these sources of energy, companies build offshore drilling platforms that bore deep into the ocean floor. When energy companies first started drilling for oil, they built rigs near the shore. Over time, however, the fossil fuel reserves in these areas dwindled. As a result, the companies had to move the rigs farther out to sea.

The first offshore oil rig in the United States was built in 1894, when Henry Williams drilled two oil wells on a California beach. A year later, he drilled another. This time the results were a bit more encouraging. Buoyed by his success, Williams built a pier 300 feet (91 meters) out into the Pacific, where he struck oil.

Workers built the first offshore "mobile" oil rig in 1947, far from land. It was located in 14 feet (4.2 meters) of water in the Gulf of Mexico just off the Louisiana coast. Today, oil rigs dot the marine landscape in the Gulf of Mexico and off the coast of California, Alaska, northeastern Canada, Cuba, and the Bahamas.

Drilling began along the eastern coast of Canada in 1967, near Nova Scotia. Oil deposits have also been discovered off Newfoundland. In the United States, however, oil and natural gas drilling is banned along the Atlantic seaboard. Oil companies have

An offshore oil-drilling rig in 1970.

Marine Resources

Gulf Coast Oil

Why is there so much oil and natural gas underneath the seabed of the Gulf Coast? The Gulf is made out of "source rocks" that formed millions of years ago from layers of algae and other tiny organisms. When the Gulf began to form, it also started to break apart. As that happened, tidal flats formed. Tidal flats are coastal wetlands that develop when rivers and tides dump mud in an area.

Algae loved the tidal flats, and over time layers upon layers of algae built up. Then the Rocky Mountains began rising from the Earth, burying the layers of algae under a massive sediment floe. Over time, these layers of algae turned into source rocks. The Earth cooked and squeezed these rocks, eventually allowing oil and natural gas to form.

An oil platform in the Gulf of Mexico, nicknamed "Devil's Tower."

been waiting for years to drill off the coast, specifically from Delaware to Florida. After the oil spill in the Gulf of Mexico in 2010, the government banned new drilling along the Atlantic seaboard until 2017.

The US Geological Survey (USGS) estimates that the US Atlantic coast could hold as much as 37 trillion cubic feet (1.04 trillion cubic meters) of natural gas and 4 billion barrels of oil. USGS officials also estimate that the National Petroleum Reserve in Alaska holds 896 million barrels of oil and 53 trillion cubic feet (1.50 trillion cubic meters) of gas, while the Gulf of Mexico could hold up to 3.8 billion barrels of oil and 21.5 trillion cubic feet (0.60 trillion cubic meters) of natural gas. While that may seem like a lot, consider that humans consume 85 million barrels of oil a day, while Americans alone use 18.6 billion barrels a day.

Wind Energy

Oil and natural gas are not the only marine sources of energy. The oceans are also a good place for wind turbines. In 2014, 3 percent of all the electricity in the United States came from wind. That's enough electricity to power 10 million houses.

The wind blows more strongly and reliably in some places than in others. One of those places is the ocean. Experts say that the amount of electricity generated from offshore wind turbines is expected to increase significantly within the next decade.

The United States is second only to China in wind-power generation. As of 2015, there were no offshore wind farms off the coast of the United States, but several were planned: one off the coast of Cape Cod; another off of Block Island, Rhode Island; and a third off the coast of Delaware.

In Canada, plans call for the construction of a $400-million 11-**megawatt** wind farm along the west coast of Newfoundland off the Gulf of St. Lawrence, and a 400-megawatt project off the northwest coast of British Columbia.

A wind farm off of the shore of Copenhagen, Denmark.

TEXT-DEPENDENT QUESTIONS

1. Which state leads in both volume and value of commercial fish?
2. How do wind farms work?
3. How many gallons of oil does the US Geological Survey estimate are under the Atlantic Ocean?

RESEARCH PROJECT

Pick one of the wind farms described in the text and write a report about it.

Chapter Four

ENVIRONMENT

March 24, 1989, was a day that will always live in infamy in Alaska. On that day, an oil tanker named the *Exxon Valdez* created one of the worst environmental disasters in history. As the ship traveled from Valdez, Alaska, to Los Angeles, California, carrying 53 million gallons of crude oil from Prudhoe Bay, its captain, Joe Hazelwood, ordered the ship's **helmsman** to maneuver away from the normal shipping lanes and go around a series of icebergs.

Words to Understand

carbonic acid: a weak acid that is created when carbon dioxide is dissolved in water.

dyslexia: a learning disorder marked by difficulty understanding written language.

genes: the basic unit of heredity that determines inherited characteristics such as eye and hair color.

helmsman: a person who steers a ship.

tsunami: a large ocean wave that is formed by an earthquake or some other tectonic activity.

Both US Navy and civilian personnel work to clean up Smith Island, Alaska, after the *Exxon Valdez* oil spill in March 1989.

The helmsman did as Hazelwood ordered. Once the ship was clear of the obstacles, Hazelwood told the ship's third mate to turn the *Valdez* back into the correct shipping lane. For some reason, however the ship never returned to its normal lane of travel. Instead, the tanker ran aground on Bligh Reef while Hazelwood was in his cabin.

The resulting oil spill was massive. The *Exxon Valdez* spilled roughly 10.9 million gallons of oil into Prince William Sound, eventually covering 1,100 miles of Alaska's pristine coastline. Then things got worse. Much worse.

At first, the oil was concentrated near the accident scene. But a day later, a storm with winds topping 70 miles (112 kilometers) per hour pounded the region, pushing the oil over a larger area. The spill traveled 90 miles (144.8 kilometers) in four days, soiling the Kenai Peninsula and Cook Inlet. Then the tide rolled in, sweeping the oil farther onshore, way beyond the usual tidal boundary.

The spill would eventually cover 11,000 square miles. Alaska's fishing industry was decimated for years. Thousands of animals died in the most grotesque ways.

Birds froze to death because the oil covered their feathers, which normally acted as an insulating blanket. Others drowned. Some animals swallowed toxic hydrocarbons. The environmental effects of the *Exxon Valdez* oil spill were still felt years after the disaster. Traces of oil remained in the region 10 years after the spill.

Interestingly, most of the oil that makes its way into the ocean does not come from major oil spills such as the 2010 explosion in the Gulf of Mexico or the *Exxon Valdez* disaster. The National Academy of Sciences says tanker or pipeline spills contribute less than 8 percent of the 29 million gallons of petroleum that enter the oceans around North America each year. The academy says nearly 85 percent comes instead from land-based runoff, polluted rivers, airplanes, small boats, and other watercraft. Another 47 million gallons seep up from the ocean floor.

A Dumping Ground

For centuries, humans have used the oceans as a dumping ground. Toxic oil spills, chemical contamination, and pollution runoff from the shore are just a few ways we

Plastic in the Ocean

Twenty percent of the plastic in the ocean is dumped by ships and offshore platforms. Plastics are not biodegradable. In other words, they don't break down into harmless substances. Experts say plastics have killed more than 100,000 sea turtles and countless fish and birds when they ingest bits of plastic or become entangled in plastic containers. The toxins from the plastic eventually seep into the food chain.

A dead albatross with a belly full of plastic trash.

have soiled the oceans. Sometimes the pollution is accidental. For example, when a devastating **tsunami** struck Japan in 2011, the water eventually washed back into the sea, creating a floating debris field the size of the Texas. Five million tons of rubbish, including wood, steel, boats, homes, cars, and trucks, washed into Pacific and moved towards North America. Mounds of debris eventually reached California.

Nevertheless, human activities are mainly to blame for the declining health of the seas. Not only have we dumped garbage, chemicals, medical waste, household trash, and human sewage into the oceans, but people also dump radioactive materials and superheated water used to cool power plants. All this pollution, coupled with global warming, is destroying marine ecosystems around the world.

Debris floating offshore of Japan after the 2011 tsunami.

Global Warming's Impact

Global warming occurs when the sun's radiation is trapped close to Earth's surface by greenhouse gases. While some of these gases, including carbon dioxide, occur naturally, the burning of fossil fuels increases their level in the atmosphere. As the amount of greenhouse gases increases, the Earth warms.

Humans add about 4.4 billion tons of carbon dioxide into the atmosphere each year. As a result, temperatures across the planet have increased nearly 1°F (0.6°C) over the last century. Every time we turn on a light, drive a car, or power up our computers, we are contributing to global warming by using electricity generated mainly by fossil fuels.

The temperature increase is also warming the oceans and slowly melting the polar ice caps, which cause sea levels to rise. The tiny Alaskan town of Shishmaref, on Sarichef Island, is on the front lines of the global warming battle. Sea ice once protected the small village from damaging floods and storm-driven waves. Warming temperatures, however, have destroyed the ice barrier, forcing residents to leave for the mainland in an attempt to escape the rising seas.

Scientists say if the current rate of ice melt continues, much of the East Coast of the United States—including New York City—will be underwater in several hundred years. The projections vary, but some scientists estimate the sea levels will rise by 13 feet (4 meters) by the year 2100. While some scientists say the increase won't be that high, a rise of 20 inches (50 centimeters) will have a dramatic impact on coastal cities.

Coral on the Brink

Coral reefs, the colorful underwater forests, are extremely vulnerable to warming temperatures and pollution. When corals are stressed by changes in the environment, they expel the algae that nourish them. When that happens, coral polyps turn white. It's a process called coral bleaching.

About 20 percent of the world's coral reefs are effectively dead because of coral bleaching. One of the largest destructions of coral occurred in 2005, when United States lost half of its coral reefs in the Caribbean when warm water near the Virgin Islands crept southward.

Bleached coral off Islamorada, Florida. When corals become stressed, they expel the algae that gives them their color, leading to this bleached appearance.

Oceanic Acidification

Since 2000, scientists have been measuring the acidity of the seaweed off Tatoosh Island near the coast of Washington State. What they have found has shocked them. Researchers have reported that the acidity of the oceans has increased tenfold from their earlier projections.

The phenomenon known as oceanic acidification has become a big problem. Oceans naturally absorb carbon dioxide (CO_2) from the atmosphere. As that happens, it increases the acidity of seawater by creating **carbonic acid**. Although carbonic acid is weak, over time it eats away at the shells and skeletons of corals, sea urchins, and stony seaweed, which impacts shell growth and the ability of some fish to reproduce. In the case of coral, carbonic acid leads to coral bleaching.

For tens of thousands of years, the oceans kept the planet's carbon cycle in balance by storing large amounts of carbon from the atmosphere. The carbon cycle is the process through which carbon moves between the land, the atmosphere, and the oceans. As long as the oceans were able to store carbon adequately, their acidity level was kept in check. That all began to change during the Industrial Revolution in the 1800s, when people began building machines and factories to make goods and products that people wanted. To power these machines, factories first burned coal, and then oil, which increased the amount of carbon dioxide in the atmosphere. Scientists say that since the beginning of the Industrial Revolution, human activities have released about 500 billion tons of carbon dioxide into the atmosphere. Consequently, the oceans have been absorbing more CO_2 than they normally would, throwing their chemistry out of balance.

The increase in acidity is affecting the marine food web, including causing the demise of plankton and shellfish. The food that plankton eat cannot survive in oceans that are warmer and more acidic. As a result, the plankton population is on the decline.

The disappearance of plankton has led to a decrease in fish that eat plankton. The birds that eat the fish are also in danger. In addition, acidification has caused sea urchins to grow slower and thinner, which makes them more vulnerable to predators. The eggs of some fish species are also threatened.

Mercury in the Oceans

No one really likes the dogfish. Some people, especially New England fishermen, call it a "trash fish." That's because no one wants to eat dogfish and it's not worth a fisherman's time to catch.

But some school districts, prisons, and homeless shelters in New England have dogfish and other so-called trash fish, such as redfish, scup, and sea robin, on their menus. Although the fish are inexpensive, many people argue

Carbon Sponge

The oceans absorb nearly 33 percent of all the CO_2 humans create, which is roughly 22 million tons a day. The increase in CO_2 means that the oceans are starting to choke on carbon and cannot soak up the gas as fast as they should. Accordingly, the oceans are losing their ability to ease the effects of global warming.

against serving or eating them. Their reason: trash fish, including dogfish, contain high levels of mercury. Mercury is a highly toxic element that can affect a person's immune system, **genes**, and nervous system. It's been linked to birth defects in children, **dyslexia**, anxiety, and other disorders. It can cause intellectual disability and memory loss in children.

The US Federal Drug Administration says that 19 dogfish species have moderate amounts of mercury in their systems, roughly 0.5 parts per million, which is some 50 times higher than clams, shrimp, and tilapia. In addition, some non-"trash fish," such as tuna, swordfish, salmon, pollock, and haddock, also contain high levels of mercury.

Mercury occurs naturally in sea water. The problem is that the level of mercury has risen in the oceans—and ultimately the food chain—due to sewer sludge and runoff from factories and landfills. Scientists have found high mercury levels in

Dogfish captured by a trawler off the coast of California.

saltwater fisheries, especially in Florida, the Gulf of Mexico, and the Atlantic waters off the coast of Canada and New England.

Mercury builds up in a person's body over time. Studies show that people who eat some types of fish from the Gulf Coast once a week have dangerously high levels of mercury in their systems. Studies also show that fish that feed near offshore oil rigs have higher levels of mercury than fish in other areas.

Dirty Fish Farms

As discussed in chapter two, aquaculture, or fish farming, is becoming increasingly more important as the planet tries to come to grips with an ever-growing population and an ever-dwindling food supply. But marine fish farming is rough on the environment. Fish farmers use massive amounts of chemicals such as antibiotics and pesticides in the process. These chemicals can find their way into the environment.

Moreover, diseases and parasites often pass between farmed-raised fish and wild fish species. When that happens, wild fish can die, dramatically altering an ecosystem. Moreover, fish farms use a lot of food, which leads to an increase in the level of fish waste. As fish waste builds up, so do the levels of nutrients in the water. When those nutrients, especially nitrogen and phosphorus, build up, oxygen becomes depleted, impacting aquatic life, including plants.

TEXT-DEPENDENT QUESTIONS

1. How much oil seeps out of the oceans naturally?
2. How does mercury find its way into the ocean?
3. How much CO_2 do human activities, such as burning fossil fuels, pour into the environment?

RESEARCH PROJECT

Many communities and states have banned people from eating certain species of fish from specific waterways because of pollution problems. Create a list of fish that you cannot eat in your state or city. List the reasons why these fish are banned, and where the sources of pollution come from.

Chapter Five

PROTECTION

It wasn't that long ago that humans viewed the resources of oceans as inexhaustible. But destructive fishing practices, pollution, acidification, and climate change have altered our perception of the briny deep. Yes, we have abused the oceans. Still, many people are working hard to protect the oceans, especially those that surround North America.

Words to Understand

archaeological: relating to archaeology, the study of ancient cultures through ancient material remains, such as buildings and other artifacts.

oceanographer: a scientists who studies the oceans.

parliament: the lawmaking body of certain countries.

Protecting the oceans is essential. As noted earlier, the oceans generate half the oxygen we breathe and provide us with one-sixth of the protein that we consume. Oceans absorb carbon dioxide from the atmosphere, regulate weather patterns, and reduce the impact of climate change.

Marine Protected Areas

The governments of Canada, the United States, and Mexico, along with those in Caribbean, have developed so-called marine protected areas (MPAs) to safeguard and restore environmentally sensitive areas. It's an idea that goes back to the Middle Ages in Europe, when kings and princes limited access to forests and streams, which curtailed hunting and fishing in those areas.

Modern-day MPAs are closed temporarily or permanently to fishing, mining, oil drilling, and other activities. Many see the MPAs as a way to offer comprehensive protection to various coastal and shoreline ecosystems that humans have already damaged. Through various regulations and rules, MPAs are designed to alleviate stress on fish, plants, and other aquatic resources while not hurting local communities that depend on these areas for their livelihoods.

However, less than 2 percent of the world's oceans are protected, and critics charge that those that are protected are not being managed correctly. The **oceanographer** Sylvia Earle has said that 10 percent of the world's oceans should be protected.

The United States has nearly 1,800 MPAs that protect coral reefs, underwater **archaeological** sites, commercial fisheries, and tourists diving sites. Some are as small as a square mile, while others cover tens of thousands of square miles.

One of the largest MPAs is the Marianas Trench Marine National Monument, home of the deepest spot on the planet. Situated near the Philippines, this US monument protects 95,216 square miles (246,608 square kilometers) of water and underwater landscapes, including volcanoes. President Barack Obama created the monument when he signed a Presidential Proclamation in 2009.

Canada also has many marine protected areas, including Gilbert Bay, located on Labrador's southeast coast. The bay is home to many different marine species,

Chapter Five: Protection 49

Maug Islands, part of the Marianas Trench Marine National Monument.

including mussels, scallops, sea urchins, and cod. The Mexican government has protected many marine ecosystems, ranging from mangrove forests, to barrier islands, to seagrass meadows.

Passing Laws

Governments also pass laws to protect small parts of the ocean. In 2000, for example, the United States passed the Coral Reef Conservation Act to preserve the country's coral reefs. The goal is to understand reef work and what threatens them. The law established four major programs. They include:

- *The National Coral Reef Action Strategy* was set up to develop research, monitoring, and conservation goals.

Ecology on the High Seas

Some cruise ship companies are educating their passengers on the seas and how not to harm habitat and wildlife. Topics covered include what makes marine protected areas so important, and how to visit the ocean without being destructive.

A tourist cruise through Antarctica.

- *The Coral Reef Conservation Program* authorizes the National Oceanic and Atmospheric Administration (NOAA), among other government agencies, to fund nonprofit organizations to study, conserve, manage, and understand coral reef systems.
- *The Coral Reef Conservation Fund* provides financial assistance for coral reef projects.
- *The National Program* makes sure the public is aware about the dangers and benefits of coral reefs. The National Program also makes sure state, local, and federal governments are working together to protect coral reefs.

Like the United States, Canada and Mexico have their own laws to protect the oceans. The Arctic Waters Pollution Prevention Act was passed the **Parliament** of Canada in 1970 to protect the Arctic waters close to the Canadian border. Among other things, the law makes it illegal for people and companies to dump any type of waste into the Arctic Ocean.

Changing Fishing Practices

Changing how people fish is another way to protect the oceans. Commercial fishing boats often use massive trawl nets to catch certain fish. Like undersea bulldozers, these trawlers scoop up everything they come across in heavily weighted nets. These nets destroy coral, oyster, and other shellfish beds.

Moreover, trawler nets rake the bottom of the seafloor indiscriminately, snaring marine mammals, sea turtles, and billions of pounds of unwanted fish. Most of these creatures, dead and alive, are simply tossed back into the ocean, creating environmental problems. When dead fish decay, for example, they decompose, creating oxygen-depleting nutrients. For every pound of fish a shrimp boat catches, fishermen toss back between 5 and 10 pounds (about 2 to 4 kilograms) of dead marine animals.

Over the years, many governments and organizations have tried to ban ocean trawlers. Dozens of countries, including Canada and China, have established no-trawl zones off their territorial waters. The United States has banned bottom trawling off most of the Pacific and Atlantic coasts. Fishermen in many areas question the effectiveness of no-trawl zones.

Sustainable Fishing

Fish are a finite resource, and humans have been overfishing for years. In fact, humans remove about 170 billion pounds (77 billion kilograms) of marine life from the oceans each year.

In order to combat overfishing, many people are turning to sustainable fishing methods. Such methods include fishing with a hook and line; using harpoons to catch larger fish, such as swordfish, without catching unwanted species; using pots and traps that don't harm the environment; fishing for specific species only during certain times of the year; and not fishing along coral reefs.

Sunset at a sustainable shrimp (prawn) farm in Queensland, Australia.

An oiled Northern Gannet is cleaned after the oil spill in the Gulf of Mexico, 2010.

Promoters of sustainable fishing also try to reduce the demand for overfished species by letting consumers know it is more beneficial to eat fish products produced by sustainable fisheries. For example, hundreds of American chefs promoted a campaign to reduce the consumption of Chilean sea bass, hoping to give the bass population time to recover. Some people even suggest not eating seafood until humans figure out better ways to protect the resource.

Banning Offshore Drilling

Soon after the 2010 Gulf Coast oil disaster, the US government banned offshore drilling in the eastern Gulf of Mexico and along the East Coast. In January 2015, the Obama administration also moved to make several areas of the Arctic Ocean off limits to drilling for five years by declaring the Arctic National Wildlife Refuge in northeastern Alaska a wilderness.

Banning offshore oil drilling is a controversial concept. Those who want to drill say the more oil America produces, the less oil the country will have to import from overseas. Moreover, drilling will create much-needed jobs—up to 280,000 jobs if the Atlantic coast was opened to drilling, according to one estimate.

Opponents of drilling say there's no need to tap into supplies of oil under the seafloor. For one thing, new technologies have made it easier to find oil on land.

> **Things You Can Do**
>
> You can help protect the oceans. Here are a few things you can do:
> - Be mindful of the amount of energy you use at home and at school. Walk when you can, or carpool with your friends. Replace old light bulbs with new energy-efficient bulbs.
> - Don't drink from plastic bottles, which can find their way into the ocean when you toss them out. Plastic kills fish and other sea creatures. Reduce your environmental footprint by recycling cans, newspapers, and other products. Don't buy coral jewelry, tortoiseshell hair accessories, or products made from shark (don't order shark fin soup at a restaurant, for example). If you don't buy these products, you'll help reduce the need for them, which will ultimately help the oceans.
> - Support or volunteer for a national organization that works to protect the oceans, especially if you live near the coast. If you ever find yourself out on a boat, never throw anything overboard, and always be aware of the marine life around you.
> - Educate yourself on the oceans and what can harm them. Share your knowledge with other people.

In addition, people say drilling in the ocean damages the environment, endangers aquatic life, and can harm coastal areas that rely on tourists.

The Role of Various Groups

Many groups, universities, and scientists are working overtime to protect the oceans by pushing various governments to enact legislation to protect marine resources. The United States leads the way by protecting nearly 10 percent of the oceans in its jurisdiction, while Great Britain is a close second. Other countries, including the other members of the G20 (the world's 20 largest economies), protect less than 1 percent of the ocean in their control

Organizations like Greenpeace, the World Wildlife Fund, and the National Resources Defense Council have taken it upon themselves to force governments into action. But you don't have to be a politician or a member of an environmental group to help save the oceans.

TEXT-DEPENDENT QUESTIONS

1. Explain how marine protected areas work.
2. Name three things you can do to help the oceans.
3. Explain the various parts of the Coral Reef Conservation Act.

RESEARCH PROJECT

Create a photo collage of the different varieties of life that are endangered in the ocean. Write a caption for each.

"To waste, to destroy, our natural resources, to skin and exhaust the land instead of using it so as to increase its usefulness, will result in undermining in the days of our children the very prosperity which we ought by right to hand down to them amplified and developed."

—Theodore Roosevelt
President of the United States (1901 to 1909)
Seventh Annual Message
December 3, 1907

Further Reading

BOOKS

Knowlton, Nancy. *Citizens of the Sea: Wondrous Creatures from the Census of Marine Life*. Washington, DC: National Geographic. 2010.

MacQuitty, Miranda. *Oceans*. DK Eyewitness Books. New York: DK Publishing, 2014.

Parker, Steve. *Seashore*. Rev. ed. DK Eyewitness Books. New York: DK Publishing, 2004.

ONLINE

Greenpeace. http://www.greenpeace.org.

Lollar, Kevin. "Sanibel Islands' Mangroves Make Comeback in Clam Bayou." *News-Press.com*, December 14, 2014. http://www.news-press.com/story/news/local/2014/12/14/sanibel-islands-mangroves-make-comeback-clam-bayou/20405221/.

Marine Conservation Institute. http://www.marine-conservation.org.

National Oceanic and Atmospheric Administration. http://www.noaa.gov.

Smith, Matt. "Empty Nets in Louisiana Three Years after the Spill." *CNN*, April 29, 2013. http://www.cnn.com/2013/04/27/us/gulf-disaster-fishing-industry/.

Series Glossary

alloy: mixture of two or more metals.

alluvial: relating to soil that is deposited by running water.

aquicludes: layers of rocks through which groundwater cannot flow.

aquifer: an underground water source.

archeologists: scientists who study ancient cultures by examining their material remains, such as buildings, tools, and other artifacts.

biodegradable: the process by which bacteria and organisms naturally break down a substance.

biodiversity: the variety of life; all the living things in an area, or on Earth on the whole.

by-product: a substance or material that is not the main desired product of a process but happens to be made along the way.

carbon: a pure chemical substance or element, symbol C, found in great amounts in living and once-living things.

catalyst: a substance that speeds up a chemical change or reaction that would otherwise happen slowly, if at all.

commodity: an item that is bought and sold.

compound: two or more elements chemically bound together.

constituent: ingredient; one of the parts of a whole.

contaminated: polluted with harmful substances.

convection: circular motion of a liquid or gas resulting from temperature differences.

corrosion: the slow destruction of metal by various chemical processes.

dredge: a machine that can remove material from under water.

emissions: substances given off by burning or similar chemical changes.

excavator: a machine, usually with one or more toothed wheels or buckets that digs material out of the ground.

flue gases: gases produced by burning and other processes that come out of flues, stacks, chimneys, and similar outlets.

forges: makes or shapes metal by heating it in furnaces or beating or hammering it.

fossil fuels: sources of fuel, such as oil and coal, that contain carbon and come from the decomposed remains of prehistoric plants and animals.

fracking: shorthand for hydraulic fracturing, a method of extracting gas and oil from rocks.

fusion: energy generated by joining two or more atoms.

geologists: scientists who study Earth's structure or that of another planet.

greenhouse gas: a gas that helps to trap and hold heat—much like the panes of glass in a greenhouse.

hydrocarbon: a substance containing only the pure chemical substances, or elements, carbon and hydrogen.

hydrologic cycle: events in which water vapor condenses and falls to the surface as rain, snow, or sleet, and then evaporates and returns to the atmosphere.

Series Glossary

indigenous: growing or living naturally in a particular region or environment.

inorganic: compound of minerals rather than living material.

kerogens: a variety of substances formed when once-living things decayed and broke down, on the way to becoming natural gas or oil.

leachate: liquid containing wastes.

mineralogists: scientists who study minerals and how to classify, locate, and distinguish them.

nonrenewable resources: natural resources that are not replenished over time; these exist in fixed, limited supplies.

ore: naturally occurring mineral from which metal can be extracted.

ozone: a form of oxygen containing three atoms of oxygen in a molecule.

porous: allowing a liquid to seep or soak through small holes and channels.

primordial: existing at the beginning of time.

producer gas: a gas created ("produced") by industrial rather than natural means.

reclamation: returning something to its former state.

reducing agent: a substance that decreases another substance in a chemical reaction.

refine: to make something purer, or separate it into its various parts.

remote sensing: detecting and gathering information from a distance, for example, when satellites in space measure air and ground temperature below.

renewable: a substance that can be made, or a process used, again and again.

reserves: amounts in store, which can be used in the future.

runoff: water not absorbed by the soil that flows into lakes, streams, rivers, and oceans.

seismology: the study of waves, as vibrations or "shaking," that pass through the Earth's rocks, soils, and other structures.

sequestration: storing or taking something to keep it for a time.

shaft: a vertical passage that gives miners access to mine.

sluice: artificial water channel that is controlled by a value or gate.

slurry: a mixture of water and a solid that can't be dissolved.

smelting: the act of separating metal from rock by melting it at high temperatures

subsidence: the sinking down of land resulting from natural shifts or human activities.

sustainable: able to carry on for a very long time, at least the foreseeable future.

synthesis: making or producing something by adding substances together.

tailing: the waste product left over after ore has been extracted from rock.

tectonic: relating to the structure and movement of the earth's crust.

watercourse: a channel along which water flows, such as a brook, creek, or river.

Index

(page numbers in *italics* refer to photographs and illustrations)

accidental pollution, 40
acidity of seawater. *See* ocean acidification
Alaska
    Exxon Valdez disaster, environmental damage, 37–39
    National Petroleum Reserve, 34
    protection of marine resources, 53–54
    Town of Shishmaref, sea level rise, 41
algae, 19–20
    biotoxins, 18, 20
    chlorophyll, 18, 19
    oil and natural gas, formation of, *34*
algal bloom, *19*, 20
Antarctic Ocean, 12, *50*
aquaculture. *See* fish farming
Arctic National Wildlife Refuge (Alaska), 53
Arctic Ocean, 12
    offshore drilling ban, 53–54
    protection laws, 51
    watersheds, 22–23
Arctic Waters Pollution Prevention Act (Canada), 51
asteroids, 12, 13
Atlantic Ocean, 12
    commercial fishing, 51
    deepest point, 12
    estuaries, 23
    mercury in the ocean, 45
    offshore drilling ban, 33–34, 53
    Puerto Rico trench, 12
    watersheds, 22–23

Bay of Fundy (Canada), 27, *28*
bays and gulfs, formation, 13–15. *See also specific bay or gulf*
    Chesapeake Bay, formation, 13–15
    Hudson Bay watershed, 15, 22
"Big Blue Marble," *11*
biotoxins, 18, 20
bromine, mining, 30
burning fossil fuels, 41

Canada
    Arctic Waters Pollution Prevention Act, 51
    Bay of Fundy, 27, *28*
    coastlines, 12
    Gilbert Bay, marine protected area (MPA), 48–49
    Hudson Bay watershed, 15, 22
    watersheds, 22–23
    wind energy, 35
carbon cycle, 43
carbon dioxide, 7, 20, 43, 48
carbonic acid, 37, 42
Challenger Deep, Mariana Trench, 12, 13, 16
Chesapeake Bay, 13–15, 23–24
Chilean sea bass, 53
China, 35, 51
chlorophyll, 18, 19
Clam Bayou (Florida), 24
climate change, 21–22
coastlines, 12–13
cod, 27–29, *31*, 49
comets, 12, 13
commercial fisheries, marine protected areas (MPAs), 48
commercial fishing industry
    changing fishing practices, 51
    cod, 27–29, *31*, 49
    Deepwater Horizon disaster, 10
    Exxon Valdez disaster, Alaska, 38–39
    fishing methods, 29
    global warming, 28–29
    limiting access fishing grounds, 48
    no-trawl zones, 51
    overfishing, 52–53
    oysters, 9–10, *23*, 32, 51
    protection of marine resources, 28, 52–53
    sonar, 27, 29
    sustainable fishing, 52–53
    top fishing states, 29
    trawlers, 27, 29, *31*, *44*, 51
    volume and value of catch, top fishing states, 29
condensation, 9, 12
conservation suggestions, 54

Index

continental shelf, 15–16, 32
copper, mining, 12, 30
coral bleaching, 41, 42
Coral Reef Conservation Act programs (US), 50–51
Coral Reef Conservation Fund, 51
Coral Reef Conservation Program, 51
coral reefs, 20–22
   climate change, impact, 21–22
   conservation suggestions, 54
   global warming, 21, 41, 42
   mangrove swamps, 24–25
   marine protected areas (MPAs), 48
   polyps, 20, 41
   Staghorn coral, 21–22
   sustainable fishing and, 52

deepest points, oceans, 12
Deepwater Horizon disaster, 9–11
   offshore drilling ban, 33–34, 53–54
Delmarva Peninsula, 13
Denmark, wind energy, 35
"Devil's Tower" oil platform (Gulf of Mexico), *34*
dogfish, mercury in the ocean, 43–44
drilling, oil and natural gas, 33–34, 53–54
dumping grounds, oceans, 39–40
   conservation suggestions, 54
   mercury in the ocean, 43–45
   ocean acidification, 42–43
   plastics, *39,* 54
dyslexia, 37, 44

Earle, Sylvia, 48
ecosystems, 18–25
   algae, 19–20
   Chesapeake Bay, ecosystem, 23–24
   coral reefs, 20–22
   estuaries, 23–24
   mangrove swamps, 24–25
   watersheds, 22–23
   wetlands, 23–24, 34
energy
   conservation suggestions, 54
   oil and natural gas, 32–34, 41, 53–54
   wind energy, 35

environment, 37–45. *See also* global warming; pollution
   carbon dioxide, 7, 20, 43, 48
   conservation suggestions, 54
   dumping grounds, ocean, 39–45, 54
   estuaries as filters, 23–24
   fish farming, environmental impact and damage caused by, 45
   mercury in the ocean, 43–45
   ocean acidification, 42–43
   oil spills, environmental damage caused by, 9–11, 37–39
   plastics dumped into ocean, *39,* 54
   protection (*See* protection of marine resources)
erosion, reduction of, 24, 25
estuaries, 23–24

first offshore oil rig, 33
fish farming, 30–32, 45
fishing. *See also* commercial fishing industry
   sport and recreational fishing industries, 30
Florida, 20, 24
fossil fuels. *See* oil and natural gas
fresh water, 15, 23–24, 29

G20, 54
Gilbert Bay (Canada), 48–49
glaciers, 13, 15, 29
global warming
   burning fossil fuels, 41
   carbon dioxide, 7, 20, 43, 48
   cod migration, 28–29
   commercial fishing industry, 28–29
   coral bleaching, 41, 42
   coral reefs, 21, 41, 42
   greenhouse gases, 41
   Gulf of Main, ecosystem, 28
   polyps, 20, 41
   sea level rise, impact and future projections, 41
gold, mining, 12, 30
Great Lakes-St. Lawrence watershed, 23
greenhouse gases, 41
Greenpeace, 54
Gulf Coast, oil and natural gas reserves, *34*

Gulf of Mexico
   bordering states and nations, 15
   Deepwater Horizon disaster, 9–11, *53*
   "Devil's Tower" oil platform, *34*
   Mississippi watershed, 22
   red tide (algal bloom), death of marine life due to, 20
   weather patterns, 15

Hazelwood, Joe, 37–38
Hudson Bay watershed (Canada), 15, 22
human consumption of fish, fresh and frozen, 29

Indian Ocean, 12
Industrial Revolution, 43

Japan
   algal bloom, *19*
   tsunami, 40
Java trench, 12

magnesium, mining, 30
manatees, 20
mangrove swamps, 24–25, 49
Marianas Trench Marine National Monument, 48, *49*
Mariana Trench, Challenger Deep, 12, 13, 16
marine protected areas (MPAs), 48–49
marsh grass, 24
Mauna Kea (Hawaii), 16
mercury in the oceans, 43–45
Mexico
   coastlines, 12
   mangrove swamps, marine protected area (MPA), 49
   Tijuana River watershed, 23
Milbrandt, Eric, 24
mineral mining, 12, 30
Mississippi watershed, 22
"mobile" oil rig, 33
mountains, 16
mud, 16

Narragansett Bay estuary, 23
National Academy of Sciences, 39

National Coral Reef Action Strategy, 50
National Petroleum Reserve (Alaska), 34
National Program (coral protection program), 51
National Resources Defense Council, 54
natural gas. *See* oil and natural gas

Obama, Barack, 48, 53
ocean acidification, 42–43
   carbonic acid, 42
ocean floor, 9, 15–16, 39
oceanographer, 47, 48
oceans, 12–13. *See also specific ocean*
   salinity, 9, 12
   tectonic plates, 9, 13, 15
offshore drilling ban, 33–34, 53–54
offshore rigs, 33
oil, natural seeping up from ocean floor, 39
oil and natural gas
   ban on offshore drilling, 33–34, 53–54
   burning, 41
   drilling, 33–34
   formation of, *34*
   offshore rigs, 33
   reserves and estimated reserves, 32, 34
oil spills, 39
   Deepwater Horizon disaster, 9–11, *53*
   Exxon Valdez disaster, 37–39
oozes, 9, 16
overfishing, 52–53
oysters
   Chesapeake Bay, *23*
   Deepwater Horizon disaster, 9–10
   fish farms, 32
   fishing practices, 51
   water filtration, *23*

Pacific Ocean, 12–13
   algal bloom (algae), *19*
   Challenger Deep, Mariana Trench, 12, 13, 16
   coastlines, 12–13
   commercial fishing, 30, 51
   deepest point, 12, 13, 16, *49*
   Japan's tsunami, 40
   mangrove swamps, 25
   Mauna Kea (Hawaii), 16

mineral mining, 30
Tijuana River watershed (US and Mexico), 23
watersheds, 22–23
Pangaea continent, 13, 15
Panthalassa Ocean, 13
peat, 24
phytoplankton, 19–20
plankton population, 43
plastics dumped into ocean, *39*, 54
pollution
accidental pollution, Japan's tsunami, 40
burning fossil fuels, 41
conservation suggestions, 54
dumping ground, 39–45
Industrial Revolution, 43
mercury in the oceans, 43–45
ocean acidification, 42–43
plastics dumped into ocean, *39*, 54
polyps, 20, 41
population
Chilean sea bass, 53
cod, 28–29
human population growth, 45
oysters, Chesapeake Bay, *23*
plankton, 43
red tides (algal bloom), 20
trawlers, impact on fish population, 29
precious metals, 12
protection of marine resources, 47–54
Arctic Waters Pollution Prevention Act (Canada), 51
banning cod fishing, 28
banning offshore drilling, 33–34, 53–54
conservation suggestions, 54
Coral Reef Conservation Act programs (US), 50–51
fishing practices, 51
marine protected areas (MPAs), 48–49
role of various groups, 54
sustainable fishing, 52–53
Puerto Rico trench, 12

recreational fishing industry, 30
red tide (algal bloom), 20
reserves, oil and natural gas, 32, 34

salinity, 9, 12
salmon, 32, 44
salt, mining, 30
salt water
estuaries, 15, 23–24
sport fishing industry, 30
San Francisco Bay estuary, 23
Sanibel's Clam Bayou (Florida), 24
sea bass, 30, 32, 53
sea trout, 30
seaweed (Tatoosh Island, Washington), 42
Shishmaref (Alaska), sea level rise, 41
shrimp
fish farms, 32, 52
fishing practices, 51
mangrove swamps, 24
mercury level, 44
shrimp boat, Gulf of Mexico, *13*
sonar, 27, 29
sport fishing industry, 30
Staghorn coral, 21–22
sustainable fishing, 52–53

tectonic plates, 9, 13, 15
Tijuana River watershed (US and Mexico), 23
trash fish, mercury in the ocean, 43–44
trawlers, 27, 29, *31*, *44*, 51
no-trawl zones, 51

uniqueness of Earth, 11–12
US
coastlines, 12–13
wind energy, 35
US Geological Survey (USGS), 34

watersheds, 22–23
weather patterns, 7, 15, 48
wetlands, 23–24, 34
Williams, Henry, 33
wind energy, 35
World Wildlife Fund, 54

zinc, mining, 30

About the Author

John Perritano is an award-winning journalist, writer, and editor from Southbury, Connecticut. He has written numerous articles and books on history, culture, and science for publishers that include National Geographic's Reading Expedition Series and its Global Issues Series. He has also contributed to Discovery.com, *Popular Mechanics,* and other magazines and Web sites. He holds a master's degree in American history from Western Connecticut State University.

Photo Credits

Cover
Clockwise from left: Dollar Photo Club/creativenature.nl; Dollar Photo Club/T Kloster; Dollar Photo Club/underworld; Dollar Photo Club/José 16; Dollar Photo Club/Moreno Novello; Dollar Photo Club/Andrea Izzotti; Dollar Photo Club/MSPhotographic.

Interior
CSIRO Marine Research: 52.
Dollar Photo Club: 13 ChmpagnDave; 16 kuma; 22 Vladimir Melnikov; 23 volff; 25 YellowCrest 29 corund; 31 ArtbyBart; 32 MARCELO; 34 MyShotz.com; 50 pilipenkod.
iStock.com: 35 AntonyMoran.
NASA: 11; 14; 19.
National Oceanic and Atmospheric Administration: 39; 44; 49.
US Coast Guard: 10.
US Department of Energy: 33.
US Fish and Wildlife Service Southeast Region: 53 Colin White.
US Geological Survey: 42.
US Navy: 40.
Wikimedia Commons: 21 Nhobgood; 28 Wladyslaw Benutzer; 38 PH2 POCHE.